Nanoaquarium

Everything About
Purchase, Care,
and Nutrition

Jakob Geck
Ulrich Schliewen

BARRON'S

Contents

The Nanomicrocosm

Nanos are the dwarfs among aquariums: tiny tanks about 12 to 20 inches (30–50 cm) long that hold less than 9 gallons (35 L) of water. With a little knowledge and care, you can create an attractive microcosm in which tiny fishes, shrimps, and delicate plants fit in perfectly.

Explanation of Terms

When the ancient Greeks spoke the word *nanos*, they surely never thought that two thousand years later it would turn into a trendy expression. For them, *nanos* simply meant *dwarf*.

Everything *nano*?

Nowadays we are familiar with not only nanotechnology, but for the last few years also nanoaquariums. Not many people know that in the past, aquariums were much smaller in size. By current standards, they were "nano," for glass was expensive and making tanks over 20 inches (50 cm) long was expensive. There is no strict definition for a nanoaquarium, but it has become customary to refer to it as an aquarium that is smaller than the size of beginner aquarium sets, with dimensions of 24 inches long, 12 inches wide, and 12 inches deep (60 × 30 × 30 cm) and containing about 13.5 gallons (54 L). The nanotanks available in pet shops have a capacity of about 1 to 9 gallons (5–35 L).

Why a Small Aquarium?

It's very simple—Nanotanks are good places to care for small fishes, dwarf shrimps, and snails that would get lost in larger tanks. They also make it easier to meet the tiny inhabitants' special needs for water and food in their miniature world, because you need smaller amounts of everything. The nice thing about these aquariums is that they need only about the space of one sheet of legal-sized paper and fit (nearly) everywhere. And yet they offer possibilities for setup and observation comparable to large tanks—as long as the accessories are also kept small. However, the miniature tanks also have drawbacks, since the smaller volume of water reacts more quickly to errors in caregiving. Furthermore, you also have to pay closer attention to a nano than to a larger tank.

The Small World of Nanoaquariums

If you want to have a nanoaquarium, you must first decide on the shape and size. You can get tanks and accessories as an all-in-one package from pet stores, or you can assemble all the mechanical devices yourself.

The Right Size

It makes a major difference for accessories, mechanical devices, and care whether you buy a tank that holds 3 gallons or 9 gallons (12 or 35 L). Ultimately your choice depends on your desires.

Perhaps you want to focus on just one animal and one plant—a "jewel," so to speak. If so, a 3-gallon (12-L) tank will be just right. But if you feel more inclined to having a miniature symbiotic relationship in support of a natural biotope, e.g., with two fishes and several plant species, then your nano should contain at least 9 gallons (35 L). It is recommended that you avoid purchasing a tank with a capacity of less than 3 gallons (12 L), for it's not possible to care properly for even the smallest creatures in such tanks.

The magic of an attractive nanoaquarium is the product of a well-thought-out composition of compatible plants and animals.

Note: Animal welfare guidelines commonly specify no minimum size for an aquarium, but rather refer merely to accommodations "appropriate to the species." Some reports recommend a minimum volume of 13.5 gallons (54 L) for keeping ornamental fishes. Still, they specify that smaller container sizes are permissible for keeping particularly small fishes. Thus our concern is to present only species that are truly appropriate for a nano and can be cared for properly in a small tank. If you have any questions about this, consult your pet shop owner.

Complete Nano Sets

Good sets consist of glass or acrylic tanks that are between 12 and 20 inches long (30 to 50 cm; capacity of 3–9 gallons/12–35 L), and that have a multichambered inside filter, a small adjustable motorized pump, and a light with one or two 9- to 11-watt tubes in a hinged cover.

Putting Together a Nano Yourself

Pet shops offer glued glass or acrylic tanks in various standard sizes. The most common sizes (length × width × height = gross capacity in liters) are approximately 12 × 8 × 8 inches (30 × 20 × 20 cm; 3 gallons/12 L), 12 × 12 × 12 inches (30 × 30 × 30 cm; 7 gallons/27 L), 16 × 10 × 8 inches (40 × 25 × 20 cm; 7.5 gallons/30 L), and 20 × 10 × 12 inches (50 × 25 × 30 cm; 10 gallons/37.5 L). These may vary according to the maker, and your pet store will be able to help you choose the proper size. For a small extra charge you can also have an aquarium made to custom dimensions. For example, if you want to imitate a small section of stream with a long, narrow tank, your best choice will be a tank measuring 24 × 8 × 8 inches (60 × 20 × 20 cm; 6 gallons/24 L).

Essential **Accessories**

ACCESSORY	DESCRIPTION
TIMER	This is necessary for regulating lighting for a regular daily routine for animals and plants. There are analog and digital types that differ mainly in price. Note that the digital ones are not as easy to adjust.
HOSES AND BUCKETS	For water changes you need about a 5-foot (1.5-m) filter hose and a 2 ½-gallon (10-L) bucket or a 2 ½-gallon (10-L) watering can.
A WATER SUPPLY CONTAINER	Water for regular partial water changes should not come straight from the tap, but rather be kept in storage, especially in the case of purified water. Use 2½-gallon (10-L) drinking water containers with screw tops so that nothing can slosh out of them.
CATCHING DEVICES	In order to remove fishes and animals, you need two fine-mesh nets with small diameter (no larger than 4 inches/10 cm). For especially sensitive mini-fishes and young fishes, you will need a dip tube to keep the creatures from coming into contact with the air.
ALGAE REMOVAL	The best device is a rough algae sponge from a pet store, or a very small algae magnet.

The Constant Search for Balance

"What goes in must also come out." This basic tenet, which obviously also applies to aquariums, is of particular importance for the small nano tank, with its extremely small volume of water. Every nano is almost complete unto itself, and is a closed, miniature environment that is related to its surroundings only through the feeding of the fishes, water changes, and the addition and removal of gases (e.g., oxygen from the air). When you consider this, the following becomes clear: all particles of food that are not eaten, all excretions, and even dead creatures that are not immediately removed remain inside the aquarium. They are broken down through the effect of useful bacteria that are present everywhere in the substrate and in the filter, but in the process they are merely transformed into other substances that, in a dissolved state, enrich the aquarium water—depending on the intensity of feeding and the inhabitants.

The Consequence (See illustration.) The dissolved waste products (red) harm the water and must be removed, since they don't spontaneously disappear from the aquarium. The bacteria in the filter (magnifying glass, top left) transform these harmful substances into less harmful ones that are dissolved but are invisible in the water (recognizable only as the buildup of a red gleam). The only way to remove the substances from the water cycle is through a partial water change (old water flows through a hose and into a bucket; freshwater is poured in from a pitcher), with fresh, unstressed water (blue) and vegetation. The arrows in the illustration indicate the direction of the water. Even in the smallest tanks the basic tenet, which the aquarium pioneer Guido Hückstedt preached, applies: "Dirt is still dirt, even if you can't see it."

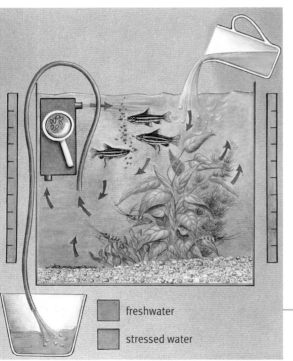

freshwater

stressed water

The substances that harm the water (red arrows) are removed from the tank through the cleansing effect of filter bacteria, plants, and water changes (blue arrows).

What Happens with Wastes in a Nano?

The main cause of dissolved waste products in the water is the proteins that are introduced with the feeding which, after initial breakdown, are present as toxic ammonia or the less poisonous ammonium. Even though high ammonium levels are not particularly harmful, they may trigger catastrophic fish deaths. For example, after a water change using tap water, the water suddenly changes into the highly toxic ammonia. Aquarium creatures react with violent breathing, but contrary to appearances, they are not suffering from a lack of oxygen but rather from ammonia poisoning.

Avoiding Ammonia Poisoning Life-threatening toxicity does not occur after every feeding, because the bacteria present in the filter and the substrate transform the resulting ammonium or ammonia further. This produces an intermediate product, such as highly toxic nitrite. This is converted by other bacteria into nitrate, which is poisonous to aquarium inhabitants only in high concentrations.

"Breaking in" the Aquarium The vitally important processes of breakdown by bacteria in the substrate and filter function in the aquarium only when sufficient quantities of bacteria have built up. This is not the case in a newly setup tank, so the few bacteria that are naturally present need to first reproduce after a new aquarium is set up.

This takes some time, generally around two to four weeks—a time that aquarium hobbyists refer to as the "break-in" phase. Even before the initial setup and operation of your nanotank, you should keep an eye on what happens during this break-in period, so that you don't put the future aquarium

Mininanos with a capacity under 3 gallons (12 L) are not suited for keeping creatures, but you can set up a beautiful tank with plants without a problem.

residents into the tank too early by mistake. The individual steps for breaking in a tank are described in detail on page 28.

Advancing at a Moderate Pace

Basic requirements for a well-functioning nanoaquarium are a moderate number of creatures, sparse feeding, and an effective filter with lots of space for the filter bacteria. This is the only way to keep an excess amount of waste substances from getting into the tank too quickly, which would not be beneficial to the health of the aquarium inhabitants. Indeed, if too much waste builds up in the aquarium, your fish could become extremely ill, and they might even die.

Basics of Nanotechnology

There is a broad selection of mechanical devices available in pet shops. Lighting, heat, and a filter are the basic accessories for every aquarium.

Lighting

Lamps for nanos may be constructed as cover lights in which the lighting element is housed under a hood that closes the aquarium up tight, except for a feeding hatch and a passageway for wires. You can also get fairly small, specially made lamps for aquariums that glue or clamp onto a

1 Lighting is important for healthy plant growth. A practical light is placed on top and folds up easily for performing maintenance chores.

2 Special nano heaters are available in pet shops. They often have a preset, integrated control and are easy to fit in with the décor.

glass side. Alternatively, you can set up a desk lamp with an energy-saving bulb and a stand beside the tank. Of course every light must meet safety requirements. If you don't use a cover light, cover the aquarium with a plate of glass so that the fishes can't jump out.

The choice of bulb depends on the nature of the lamp: a good choice is full-spectrum daylight compact fluorescent tubes with 9 to 11 watts. For an average nanoaquarium with a normal amount of animals and plants, a compact fluorescent light with one or two T5 bulbs is adequate. If you have a nano along the lines of a Japanese nature aquarium (see page 19), you will need stronger lighting. A reliable timer is essential for all aquariums (see page 7).

Heating

Wand heaters with a built-in adjustable thermostat and a performance between 10 and 25 watts are good for nanos. Heaters with higher performance must not be used, because they heat up the water too quickly and can overheat the tank. Pet shops also offer small-format nanoheaters whose thermostat is set to 77°F (25°C)—a temperature that is optimal for most tropical creatures.

If you are taking care of several nanos with the same temperature requirements, you can install a separate thermostat in one tank that will simultaneously control several heaters (without a control) in various tanks. You can also use a separate thermostat to control a heating mat placed under the tank.

Filtration

The filter serves to collect waste substances in something like a strainer (mechanical filtration), and to transform harmful waste products dissolved in the water into harmless substances (biological filtration).

Because the small volume of water in a nano-tank reacts more quickly and sensitively to errors, large-volume filters are important. The size of the filter should make up about 5 to 10 percent of the tank volume.

Several types of filters are available on the market.

› Foam cartridges, foam mats, or bubble filters are driven by airlift or minimotor pumps. These filters exhibit a high degree of effectiveness, because they provide a relatively slow water flow over a large filter surface. This gives the filter bacteria enough time to cleanse the water as it flows.

› "Hamburg mat filters," which consist of a square mat of filter foam, are particularly effective. They completely block off one corner or side of the aquarium. With minimotor pumps or airlift pumps installed behind the mat, the water is sucked through the large mat surface.

The mat filter should be slightly larger than the inside dimensions of the tank so that you can use a knife to fit it closely to the inside dimensions of the aquarium without creating any space.

› In many complete nanosets, a so-called "filter chamber" is created through a dividing wall glued into place. This can be equipped with filter materials and the mechanical devices (pump or airlift and heater).

› Motorized insider filters with small filter insert cartridges are used in slightly larger nanos. They circulate the aquarium water around quite force-fully, but on the average they provide too little filter volume.

You should choose a model that can accommodate various types of filter materials, and one that has a motor that can be throttled down.

› Piggyback outside filters are installed outside the tank. They provide a relatively large filter volume and create a fairly significant current. If you opt for this type of filter, be sure that you set up your aquarium in a place with sufficient room to accommodate the extra bulk. (See illustration below.)

3 An air-operated inside foam cartridge filter provides good water when the air input is moderate.

4 A piggyback filter with adjustable flow and a small motor pump can be used with a wide range of aquariums.

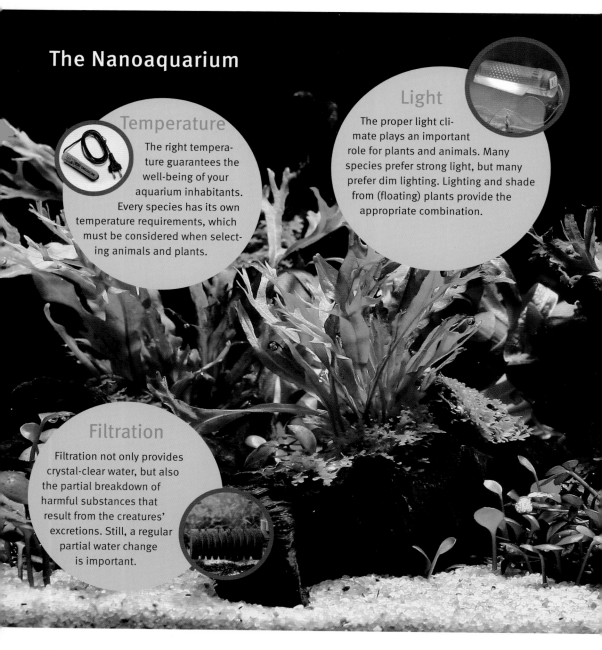

The Nanoaquarium

Temperature

The right temperature guarantees the well-being of your aquarium inhabitants. Every species has its own temperature requirements, which must be considered when selecting animals and plants.

Light

The proper light climate plays an important role for plants and animals. Many species prefer strong light, but many prefer dim lighting. Lighting and shade from (floating) plants provide the appropriate combination.

Filtration

Filtration not only provides crystal-clear water, but also the partial breakdown of harmful substances that result from the creatures' excretions. Still, a regular partial water change is important.

Creatures

Fishes and crustaceans turn a seemingly lifeless still-life into a living biotope. Only small species (dwarf fighting fishes) are appropriate choices for keeping in a minitank.

Plants

Water plants provide not only a good water climate, but also lots of hiding places for shrimps and fishes. In addition to adequate light, plants need careful fertilizing.

Substrate

The substrate offers plants and bottom-feeding fishes an important piece of habitat. Rooting plants get nutrients from a layer of fertilizer added to the bottom.

Learning About Water

Water is not just water. It may be more or less appropriate for animals and plants, depending on the dissolved substances it contains. The most important features of tap water are the hardness (calcium content) and the pH (acidic, neutral, or alkaline). Whether or not you can put tap water directly into the tank or first have to purify it depends on these values and on the requirements of the animal and plant species. It is easy to determine the most important water values with simple droplet tests or electronic measuring devices from a pet shop.

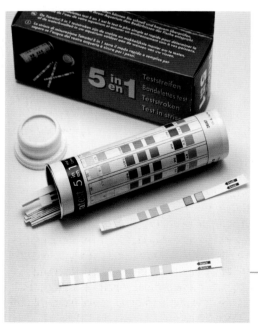

Water Hardness

What's known as water hardness is produced by salts dissolved in the water. This is measured in levels of dH. You may also encounter references to German Degrees of Hardness (°dH). With water hardness, depending on chemical composition, there is a distinction between carbonate hardness and noncarbonate hardness. The difference between these two is simple: the carbonate hardness factors can be precipitated out as calcium—that's why the calcium moves around in kettles of boiling water, for example—whereas the noncarbonate factors remain dissolved in the water. When referring to the overall hardness of the water, both are taken together.

Different Degrees of Hardness Water is divided into the following five degrees of hardness:

> very soft water   0 to 3
> soft water   3 to 7
> medium-hard water   7 to 14
> hard water   14 to 21
> very hard water   over 21

Importance for Aquarium Hobbyists The carbonate hardness is more significant for aquariums than the noncarbonate hardness, since it usually makes up the major portion of tap water. Aquarium creatures vary noticeably with respect to their tolerance for water hardness, so many species can be kept and raised in very hard water, while other

You can also use multitest strips for checking the water, but they are imprecise and are good for only a general impression.

species can live in it quite well but not reproduce in it. The most demanding species—often blackwater fishes—can be kept in only soft to very soft water (see page 16).

Water Acidity Level

Other important qualities of aquarium water are specified through the degree of acidity, that is, the content of acids and bases in the water. The acidity level is expressed as a pH, which can fall between 0 and 14. If the pH is less than 7, it is acidic water; if it exceeds a value of 7, the water is basic or alkaline. Water with a pH of 7 is neutral.

Important Producers of Acids and Bases The pH alone provides no information about which acids or bases are present, or which substances are responsible for the measured pH value. Some of the most important producers of acids and bases in nature and in an aquarium are the following:

> Carbonic acid: This results when the carbon dioxide in the water is dissolved. Carbon dioxide is an ingredient of air and gets into the water through the surface or through special aeration. Aeration that produces too many bubbles can also drive out carbon dioxide (carbonated bottle effect). Carbon dioxide is artificially added to aquarium water to provide plants with this important nutrient (see page 53).

> Humic acids: These get into the water through contact with certain plant materials, e.g., peat moss. They also give the water a yellowish tint.

> Carbonates: These are products of bases and result when the water flows through layers of rock that contain carbon, such as limestone. Such water values can vary greatly around North America, so you should check your water to develop a baseline from which to work.

The Celestial Pearl Danio has developed into a winner for nanoaquariums. This somewhat shy species needs thick vegetation to feel comfortable.

Mutual Dependence

Carbonate hardness, carbonic acid, and pH values have an effect on each another. This means that one value (e.g., carbonate hardness) cannot be changed without also changing the carbonic acid content in the water, and thus the pH value to a greater or lesser degree. It is important to recognize this interdependence if you wish to prepare water containing little carbonate hardness for soft-water fishes (see page 16), or to fertilize the plants with carbon dioxide.

How it Works Extremely soft water with no carbonate hardness (under 1° dKH) can easily be made much more acidic through small amounts of (carbonic) acid; this is known as poorly buffered water. Even very soft water should be buffered through at least a carbonate hardness of 0.5° dKH; otherwise, the pH can drop to levels that are inhospitable to fishes.

Providing the Right Water

Even tap water can be used for a nanoaquarium if the water hardness and the pH are appropriate for the creatures, and if it is not contaminated by nitrates, pesticides, or heavy metals. The reduced amount of water in a nano has a great advantage in providing for sensitive dwarf species with special water needs, because it is easier to buy and store specially prepared water in small amounts.

Storage in a Jug or Small Barrel You should keep one or two tank volumes of water appropriate for the nano in various plastic jugs or small plastic containers. In the following sections you will find out how to prepare water for your needs.

What Kind of Water for Which Requirements?

In order to find out the answer to this question, you have to know the starting point of your tap water as well as the requirements of your fish and plant

Small black alder cones contain the humic acids that change pH levels. They can be used in preparing water for a nano.

species. The profile section of this book (starting on page 32) will help you choose.

Tap water (nonchlorinated) can often be used, but it should stand overnight before use. Since water values vary by region, they must be determined individually for your specific location. Many water systems in North America also use chloramines, which cannot be removed by letting the water stand. Chemicals that remove chloramines can be obtained at your pet store if needed.

Soft and slightly acidic water is preferred by many species, because it corresponds to the natural qualities of most wild tropical waters. In addition, providing plants with carbon dioxide works better in this type of water.

Preparing Soft Water

Soft water for aquariums is made from hard, basic tap water by mixing tap water with soft water. The water can also be filtered through materials that soften it. Afterward, if the water hardness is low and the pH is still too high, acidifying substances are added to it (see page 17). Completely distilled water, which is soft and free from any hardness-forming substances such as calcium, can be obtained from various sources:

> Pet shops or building supply stores: Because of the cost, this is only appropriate for getting through emergency situations.

> Reverse osmosis system: A small device driven by the water pressure from the tap is used to produce one part completely desalinated water and three parts residual water. Buying a small reverse osmosis device for small quantities of water is cheaper over the long run than buying distilled water.

> Rain water: This is likewise free from hardness-forming substances, as long as it has not run over harmful substances on roofs and in pipes. It should be gathered only after a fairly long rainfall so that all impurities from the air are washed out. Note that the water should be filtered through activated carbon as it is put into storage containers to remove any remaining harmful substances. Rain values may vary greatly in pH, so you should check this before use.

> Ion exchanger: This filters tap water through ion exchange resins, which must be re-purified with aggressive chemicals once they become used up. This is convenient, but the regeneration requires practice in dealing with chemicals.

Calculating Mix Proportions

You can calculate the correct mix of completely desalinated water and tap water if you know the values of the tap water.

How to do it: The hardness degree of tap water (e.g., 18° dKH) minus the desired degree of hardness (e.g., 4° dKH) yields the proportion of the completely desalinated water: 18 − 4 = 14. So, for example, if you want to produce a hardened water with 0° dKH from tap water with 18° dKH, you mix four parts tap water and fourteen parts softened water.

Acidifying Soft Water

Only soft water with little carbonate hardness can be acidified successfully, because it is not as well buffered. Place the appropriate soft water into a container and acidify it with one handful of peat moss from the pet shop per 10 quarts/liters of water. Aerate the container with an air stone and measure the pH and carbonate hardness levels after a day. Keep adding until the desired values are reached.

Preparing **Black Water**

A TIP FROM THE EXPERT:
Jakob Geck

WHAT IS IT? Black water is acidic water containing few minerals that gets its dark color from humic substances. Because of the extreme water values, it contains hardly any germs. Many of the most attractive nano fishes come from blackwater biotopes (see page 32), and for breeding they continually need water values from 0–1° of carbonate hardness and a pH of around 5.

HOW DOES THIS WORK? Use completely desalinated water with no blended tap water, and gradually acidify it with oak extract from a pet shop. Aerate with an air stone and check the pH again after an hour, for it can change further with time.

NOTE The pH often changes suddenly, so dispense the oak extract carefully. Black water is produced by adding peat extracts that do not acidify the water but color it. The disadvantage of this water type is that with improper care, the acidity level can become too low. As a result, a partial water change is particularly important.

Water Plants in a Nanoaquarium

The importance of plants in an aquarium cannot be overestimated, especially in a nanotank. Healthy vegetation provides oxygen throughout the day, ties up organic wastes to a certain degree, provides a retreat for fishes, and on top of everything else, looks good. Even tiny aquariums can be beautifully transformed into a miniature jungle in which shy fishes can find plenty of hiding spots. The tank can also be set up as a type of landscape garden, e.g., in the style of a Japanese nature aquarium.

Vitally Important Nutrients

All aquarium plants need nutrients in the form of added fertilizer and carbon dioxide (CO_2), which is used for photosynthesis in the light. The type and amount of nutrients depends on how you want to set up your aquarium.

A tank with fishes and crustaceans requires average lighting and fertilizing. In this case, only moderate plant growth is appropriate; otherwise, the tank will quickly become overgrown and many

A tank planted with a variety of vegetation provides not only a healthy water climate but also a retreat for shy inhabitants.

species will grow too large. If the water values are matched to the plant species, these tanks need only occasional fertilizing.

On the other hand, the **Japanese nature aquarium** needs intense lighting and a steady supply of nutrients, for a particular "plant image" needs to be created in a short time.

Inadequate fertilizing leads to nutrient deficiency and harms the plants. Carbon dioxide fertilizing is also important for this type of aquarium (see page 53). There are special small apparatuses for nano tanks; they must be used according to the directions since they can produce an overdose of CO_2, which can be harmful to the fishes.

The Right Fertilizer

There are essentially two types of fertilizers that can be used based on the plants involved.

Substrate fertilizers are appropriate for all aquariums with a substrate and rooting plants. They are included in the bottom layer of the substrate when the tank is set up (see page 26).

Liquid fertilizers provide all species of water plants with nutrients. These fertilizers are added at every partial water change, or automatically by means of a dosator.

You will find out how to fertilize plants in a nano aquarium on page 52.

Bee shrimps like a carpet of vegetation where they can search for food.

Planted Tanks with No Substrate

It often makes sense to use only water plants, or what's known as epiphytes, which grow on wood or stones. These plants are appropriate for tanks with a sand bottom and a population of Peppered Cories, or for tanks with a leaf bottom. Liquid fertilizers are used in this type of tank.

Plant Selection and Care

Plants that remain small are the only choice for nanotanks. Make sure that their temperature and water requirements match those of the fishes and other creatures. There are, for example, plants that eventually waste away in hard water. Our profiles (see pages 20–21) will introduce you to some appropriate plants.

Nanoplants in Profile

Well-balanced planting enriches all aquariums, no matter how small they may be. On these two pages, we introduce you to some appropriate plant species that are particularly easy to care for.

JAVA MOOS *(Vesicularia dubyana)* Used as a cushion or attached to roots or stones; does not withstand fairly long stretches of temperatures over 82°F (28°C).

CRYSTALWORT *(Riccia fluitans)* A robust floating plant found worldwide, which can be attached to stones and roots with nylon thread. It needs lots of light and nutrients, and forms a thick, decorative cushion.

CRYPTOCORYNE PARVA This smallest of the crypts, which grows 1 to 2 inches (2–5 cm) high, is recognizable by the fact that it lies broadly on the substrate. This is a good choice as a foreground plant, or for tanks that don't get much light, or have fairly hard water.

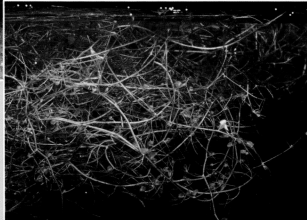

HUMPED BLADDERWORT *(Utricularia gibba)* A floating plant that tolerates extremely soft, acidic water. This is the first choice for a blackwater tank.

PYGMY CHAIN SWORD *(Echinodorus tenellus)* A decorative plant that grows to about 2 inches (5 cm) and forms a lawn for the foreground. This is used in tanks with soft to medium-hard water with a temperature of 68–82°F (20–28°C). It thrives with carbon dioxide fertilizing.

DWARF ANUBIAS *(Anubias nana)* A robust, slow-growing epiphyte that ties to roots or stones. Never place the rhizome in the substrate.

WINDELOV JAVA FERN *(Microsorum pteropus "Windelov")* A decorative, undemanding epiphyte that is a better choice for fairly large nanos. It also tolerates very soft, acidic water. Tie to roots or stones.

DOWNOI *(Pogestomon helferi)* A plant that likes strong light and is for soft to medium-hard water. It can be planted in the substrate or cultivated as an epiphyte. This species is somewhat more demanding.

The First Steps

The theoretical requirements and the technical know-how for maintaining a successful nanoaquarium were explained on the preceding pages. Now it is time to turn our thoughts to the right way to set up the tank so that the future aquarium inhabitants feel most comfortable.

Providing the Right Conditions

Different species have varying demands, which dictates how the nano is set up and maintained. The most important clues are always provided by the natural environment of the plants and creatures kept in the aquarium. You should take the following two considerations to heart.

The Right Nano for the Right Creature

A functioning nano is like a well-balanced organism: when the size, setup, mechanical devices, water quality, and feeding are well matched to the animal species, the tank turns into a microcosm. But if the balance is not right, it is nothing more than a small glass case filled with water. Getting all factors to work together requires a bit of care. To ensure that even beginners can make a successful start, we present four proven animal and plant combinations for a 6-gallon (25-L) tank starting on page 32. If you want to start off with different species, you should gather information on their care requirements, but one of the four sample nanoaquariums will probably meet your needs with only a few modifications.

Quick, Daily Care Is a Must

Nanos, more than other types of aquariums, need care. This doesn't mean that you have to spend several hours on it every day; a couple of minutes will suffice. Your tasks involve deliberate, careful feeding, checking the creatures' vitality and the proper functioning of the mechanical devices, and planning and preparing food and water for the following day. Nanocreatures are tiny, so they don't have many reserves and often have reduced resistance for getting through long breaks in care.

Natural Habitats of Nanocreatures

The most important requirement for proper living conditions is a familiarity with the natural habitats of the aquarium dwellers. Creatures for nanotanks belong to very diverse groups. What they have in common is their small body size, which enabled them to take over their habitats in the wild, which were closed to many large species. Small fishes cannot live as well as larger fishes in a strong current, because they don't have the muscle power to exert against the current. On the other hand, it is significantly easier for them to search for food in small biotopes, and to find shelter from both an excessively strong current and from their enemies—large predatory fishes for whom they would be easy prey in open water.

On the following pages we will present the most important habitats that the smallest fishes and shrimps inhabit in the wild. The descriptions can serve as the basis for imitation in the aquarium.

Weedy Still Water

When water quality and light conditions allow, thick growths of finely leafed water plants grow in most still water areas. Small ponds, ditches, and swamps may even be completely grown in.

With a water quality that hardly allows plant growth, like black water, for example (see page 17), land plants that hang into the water provide the same habitat as thickets of water plants. Schooling fishes such as Tetras and Rasboras catch small particles of food at the edge of these thickets. Always on their guard, there is always a possibility that they will pull back quickly if danger arises.

Species inclined to be loners "creep" around with slow movements through the plant undergrowth looking for small food creatures, which are found in abundance among finely leafed plants. Small catfishes equipped with a suction mouth, such as Ottos, pick algae and small living creatures from broad-leafed plants.

Under the surface of frequently swampy, oxygen-poor waters, the males of Dwarf-Fighting Fish or Sparkling Gouramies build their foam nests. *Corydoras* rummage around for worms and insect larvae in the fine, soft bottom that builds up in the root area of plant thickets.

This weedy stream is an ideal habitat for the Scarlet Badis. These fishes like shorelines with lots of structural variety.

Tiny Rain Forest Streams

Many streams have a water depth of only a few inches. Therefore, these usually clean and relatively cool waters are reserved almost exclusively for small fish species.

Such streams offer various fish and shrimp species valuable habitats.

Blue Panchax live right under the surface of the water and seize insects that fall into the water from vegetation on the shore. Other killifish species, such as the Cape Lopez Lyretail (*Aphyosemion australe*), likewise stay in protected calm water areas right under the surface of the water near the shore and wait for insects. Gobies and prawn like fallen leaves, and the Gobies use the leaves for spawning cavities.

In addition to fallen leaves, schooling fishes also use the tangled root network of trees near the water for spawning and hiding. The bottom of these streams is mostly sandy with some gravel. Catfishes and Barbs search for food in the sand.

If the lighting is not reduced too much by the trees, even in streams with a strong current, long-leafed water plants with their undulating leaves create calm water areas that nocturnal fishes and little loaches use for sleeping during the day.

Interestingly, fishes from the small, clear, rain forest streams are among the most colorful ones. With their reflective, iridescent colors, they use the little light that the crown of trees lets through to the ground to make themselves conspicuous during the courtship ritual.

Shallow Water Areas

There are also habitats in catchment areas of fairly large flowing waters in which small fishes find

A flat shore area of a blackwater stream in Thailand contains hundreds of Dwarf Rasboras among reedlike plants.

protection from enemies, as well as areas with little current and sumptuous vegetation.

In coves in the rain forest and in separate branches of a river, or in the overflow areas high above the mainstream during the rainy season, there is often a layer of fallen leaves a yard and a half (1.4 m) deep at the bottom of the water.

The fallen leaves provide the nutritional basis for many small creatures, especially shrimps.

They also function as a net for food particles drifting by slowly. During the rainy season all creatures fatten up on the sumptuous vegetation of the flooded rain forest, and swarm over broad areas and reproduce there in the same year.

The same conditions also apply to the running waters of the savannas. They leave their banks and form stagnant water areas and ponds for small killifishes such as the *Nothobranchius palmqvisti*.

A Step-by-Step Guide to Setting Up a Nano

The tank and mechanical devices are ready, the plants, substrate, and decorations are in position, and the appropriate water is waiting inside containers—the nano can now be set up and equipped.

Finding the Right Plants

Before you set up the tank, you should decide on exactly where to place the aquarium. Since the temperature can fluctuate easily in a small volume of water, a nanotank should be set up only in places with no direct sunlight and at a distance from heaters. It is equally important for it to be in a quiet place that is not subject to vibrations, such as the living room. Many species of fish are particularly timid and can easily become stressed out by too much movement close to the aquarium. Place the tank on a level surface with a flexible underlay such as Styrofoam from a pet shop or hardware store, which will even out irregularities and prevent glass breakage.

Choosing the Substrate and Decorations

If you use rooting plants on the bottom, fill the tank about 2 inches (5 cm) deep with quartz sand (river sand) or quartz gravel with no sharp edges in pieces up to 0.039 inches to 0.078 inches (1–2 mm). Add a very small amount of fertilizer to the substrate (see page 19).

If rooting plants are not used, a substrate depth of about a half inch (1 cm) is adequate. Small roots from a pet shop (driftwood and mopani wood) and small stones without calcium make good decorations.

Preparations for Setup

It's best to proceed step by step so that the setup will come out right the first time.

Wash the Substrate and Rinse the Roots and Stones. River sand and gravel contain many tiny particles that can discolor the water when the aquarium is filled with water. Therefore, it is better to wash the substrate in a bucket under running water until the water flowing out is clear.

Materials used for decorations are often dusty and dirty, so rinse them thoroughly.

Preparing the Plants. The pot and plant substrate are carefully removed from potted plants. Very long roots are trimmed to around an inch or two (3–4 cm). Newly purchased plants should be

Many dwarf fishes are comfortable with a decoration of brown autumn leaves.

disinfected in an alum bath for around 20 minutes (1 teaspoon of alum salts from the drugstore in 1 quart/ 0.9 L of water). This prevents the introduction of snails and parasites. After the bath, thoroughly rinse the plants. Epiphyte (non-rooted) plants are tied to stones or roots with nylon line, black cotton thread, or even hair nets (for cushions of moss) so that they don't float away.

Getting the Mechanical Devices Ready. All devices should be assembled according to the instructions so that they are ready for use.

Sketching the Vegetation and Decorations. It is very helpful to do a preliminary sketch of how the plants and objects will be grouped together.

By following these steps, you avoid unnecessary disruptions through repeated redecorating later on

STEP ONE Depending on the plants selected, put in about a half inch to 2 inches (1–5 cm) of washed substrate, and add fertilizer to the bottom layer. Smooth out the substrate with your hand or a spatula. Position the prepared decorations with the attached epiphyte plants by pushing them firmly into the substrate. Install the mechanical devices so that they are ready to be turned on for use.

STEP TWO Put a cup on the bottom and pour water into it so that the substrate does not swirl around. Use tweezers to insert creeping plants a short distance from one another; plant stem plants along the tank sides or in the background, and fairly large rosette plants in central locations. Fill up the tank and turn on the mechanical devices.

STEP THREE During the following weeks the tank is in the break-in phase (see page 28). While the plants are taking root and the bacteria in the filter and substrate are reproducing, not much should be done in the tank. Only when the break-in phase is over should fishes and other creatures be placed in the tank (see page 44).

after the creatures have moved in. With respect to the plants, you should take into account the different shapes and growing speeds: *Cryptocoryne, Anubias*, and Java Ferns grow relatively slowly, but carpet-forming plants and stem plants quickly grow tall.

› Carpet-forming species are placed individually in the foreground an inch or less (1–2 cm) apart from one another; they will soon form a unified surface.

› Put in taller plants in such a way that they are freestanding and have a little extra room for further growth; nothing looks less attractive than a solitary plant "squished" into a corner.

› Epiphyte plants, in contrast to plants with roots, can easily be moved along with their substrate to create the best overall impression.

The Break-in Phase—the Most Important Step

Once the aquarium is set up and put into operation, it must be "broken in." During the first two to four weeks your aquarium will become biologically active; that is, useful and important bacteria strains in the filter and substrate are gradually building up, since they are not present from the outset.

The break-in phase proceeds with the following steps:

› On the day the aquarium is set up it is nearly dead biologically. At this point there are hardly any useful bacteria in the substrate and filter.

› As soon as a day later, there is toxic decomposed material in the water from the tiniest quantities of organic waste products, e.g., rotten plant material. On the second day there are more harmful substances, especially nitrite, which is highly toxic to fishes and shrimps. There is still not enough bacteria present to neutralize these toxic substances in the aquarium.

› After two to three weeks the bacteria have reproduced to the point that they can transform the harmful substances into less harmful nitrate.

› After two to three weeks, when no further nitrite can be detected using water test kits from a pet shop, it can be assumed that the self-cleaning capability of the tank has stabilized. Now fishes and other creatures can be placed in the tank.

› From this point on, conduct regular nitrite checks, at least every three days.

› Once the break-in phase of three to four weeks is over, a partial water change of a quarter to a third of the water at least once a week is essential; otherwise, nitrates and other substances will build up.

Shortening the Break-in Process

As you can see, the break-in phase takes time. There are various tricks for increasing the number of bacteria right from the outset; you can either put in used filter material from a functioning tank, or use so-called "filter starters" from pet shops. Another method also promises success: put a handful of unfertilized, unstressed dirt into a container, add 1 quart (0.9 L) of water, stir it up, and let it sit for two or three hours. If the water is clear, pour it through a strainer into the nano so that no dirt gets in. These tricks will shorten the break-in phase to about one week.

TIED PLANTS Epiphyte plants such as Java Fern, moss, and giant *Anubias* use tiny prehensile organs to grow on solid substrates. Until that point, though, you will have to tie them on with nylon, cotton thread, or a hair net so that they don't float away. It will take a few weeks before you can remove the unsightly thread. Materials that decompose, such as cotton thread, have the advantage of not having to be removed.

STONES AND ROOTS come in a broad selection in aquarium shops. Don't buy any that will over-power your tank. Before you put them into the aquarium, rinse and clean them or boil them in a pot. Don't use any roots from the forest that could still decay. Stones should be free of calcium. To test them, drip essence of vinegar onto a rock; if it foams, it contains calcium.

CAVES FOR HIDING Many fishes love caves made from untreated bamboo tubes, homemade or factory-made clay pipes, hollowed coconut shell halves, and even plastic pipes.

A Nanoaquarium in Profile

There are many ways to set up a nanotank in an appropriate and asthetically pleasing way. The most important guideline is the requirements of the inhabitants with respect to water quality, setup, and—in case several species are kept—compatibility with one another. In the following pages we present four types of nanoaquariums and provide tips on setup, planting, and care. We mention at least three species of creatures for each type that are especially well suited to the type of nano pre-sented. All the information in the profiles refers to a 6-gallon (24-L) aquarium. Some species need a larger tank (e.g., schooling fishes), so this is noted as well. In a 3-gallon (12-L) nano, you should always keep just one species.

Selecting the Right Creatures

Pet shops offer several hundred species of fishes and crustaceans, but only a fraction of them are suited for a nanoaquarium. How do you choose the right ones?

Nanotanks can be set up in a wide variety of places in your home. It's best to choose a quiet location and to avoid placing the tank on a windowsill or close to a heating element.

> Choose only species that will remain very small. The creatures should grow to be no longer than about 1.5 inches (3.5 cm)—in 3-gallon/12-L nanos, it's best to stick to about an inch or slightly larger (2.5–3 cm); they should be calm swimmers rather than frantic or easily startled; and they should have no major territorial requirements. Many species that are suited for nanoaquariums have names preceded by the designation *dwarf* or *pygmy*.

> Find out about what kinds of care the fishes require if you want to get species that are not included in this book. Make sure you can provide the proper water conditions. Fishes for soft or black water need prepared water, because it generally doesn't come from the tap in the quality required. Feeding requirements also vary significantly.

> Don't choose fishes and shrimps based only on their colorful appearance. Many species are distinguished by their particular behaviors, which sometimes are exhibited only at such times as the mating season. This adds a variety of behaviors to your tank. You will surely watch with enthusiasm as the male Sparkling (or Pygmy) Gourami builds a foam nest for the eggs and plays around with clearly perceptible purring sounds.

> In all cases avoid putting in too many fishes. The information in the profiles will help you to determine the maximum number of individuals to place in your tank. Remember: less is always better.

> If you want to keep more than one species in a fairly large nano (6 gallons/25 L or larger), compare the care requirements for all the desired species to make sure they are compatible. Always put in a bottom-dwelling species with a species that prefers the middle or upper water layers. A nanotank is too small for keeping two species that use the same section of water.

Meeting **Shelter Requirements**

A TIP FROM
THE EXPERT:
Ulrich Schliewen

WHY SHELTER? In the wild, most fishes have enemies and are therefore continually on guard against possible attacks. Fishes captured in the wild often react fearfully to activities outside the aquarium, so provide them with shelter to reduce their jumpiness.

RETREAT Provide adequate opportunities for a retreat, such as thick planting around the edge and a layer of floating water plants. The latter satisfies the important need for protection from anticipated enemies from the air, such as birds that eat fishes. Provide small sheltered areas consisting of roots, stones, and hollows for bottom dwellers. Creatures that can flee to such sheltered areas are more inclined to show themselves in the open swimming area, since they can always retreat in case of doubt.

BRAVE EXAMPLES Put shy species in with species that are not timid. In fairly large nanos (6 gallons/25 L or larger) you can put in fishes for the middle and lower levels such as Celestial Pearl Danios with carefree upper-level species such as Clown Killifishes.

South American Nano

South America's rain forest is home to the greatest variety of freshwater fishes in the world. It's no wonder that this is where most pygmy fish species live. A large number come from nutrient-poor forest or savanna streams that contain slightly to highly acidic water. These running waters are—at least during the dry season—crystal clear and contain lots of water plants. If the water also has a brownish hue, it is referred to as black water (see page 17). In general, it is characterized by significantly reduced plant growth.

Species The most popular species from South America come from the groups of characins and *Corydoras*, which can be put together only in fairly large nano tanks of 9 gallons (35 L) or larger. In addition, in South America there are small killifishes from the genus *Rivulus*, which are similar to the Cape Lopez Lyretail from Africa (see page 35).

Setup More than other types of nanos, the South American nano takes on life from the colorful interplay of the schooling fishes or *Corydoras* with the sumptuous South American water plants. One setup variation involves combining a substrate of fine gravel with grasslike sword plants and water plants. The decoration can be started with one small root and epiphyte plants. Colorful characins use the grasslike sword plants as a place of retreat, and the males set up tiny territories in the spaces among the plants. If you want to keep bottom-dwelling *Corydoras*, instead of the gravel substrate, you need a sand bottom with sparser planting so there is adequate space for foraging.

Stocking The following basic rule applies: in a 3-gallon (12-L) nano, only one species is kept. In a 6-gallon (25-L) tank, that species can be kept along with a trio of Ottos (*Otocinclus*). These catfishes help with algae control. If the aquarium has a capacity of at least 9 gallons (35 L), you can keep two species plus a trio of Ottos.

Particulars If you have Ottos in your nano, you must also provide the creatures with additional green dry food, for the algae alone are not sufficient.

Nannostomus marginatus
Dwarf Pencilfish

Approximately 1.5 inches (3.5 cm). **Origin** Still water fish that lives in the Amazon in bodies of water with abundant plant life. **Care** Soft, slightly acidic water (pH 6–6.5); 72–79°F (22–26°C). Thick vegetation with room to swim between. Keep seven fishes: three males and four females. Eats small live food, e.g. *Artemia* nauplii; also gets used to consuming frozen food and dried plant food. **Socialization** In 6 gallons (25 L) with three *Otocinclus* catfishes; in 9 gallons (35 L), additionally with twelve Ember Tetras. **Similar** *Nannostomus* sp. "purple," 1.5 inches (3.5 cm).

Hyphessobrycon amandae
Ember Tetra

One-half inch (1 cm). **Origin** Black water regions in southern Brazil. **Care** Soft, acidic water (pH 5–6); 75–83°F (24–28°C). Red coloration occurs only in soft, acidic water filtered with peat. Dark substrate with thick vegetation. Schooling fish, so keep at least twelve fishes. Feed small types of food (e.g., Cyclops, *Artemia* nauplii, dried food). **Socialization** With three *Otocinclus* catfishes in 6-gallon (25-L) tank; in 9 gallons (35 L) with six freshwater catfishes (e.g., *Aspidoras pauciradiatus*). **Similar** Green Neon Tetra (*Paracheirodon simulans*), 1.5 inches (3.5 cm).

Corydoras habrosus
Dainty Cory

1.2 inches (3 cm). **Origin** Sandy streams in Venezuela. **Care** Soft to hard water, pH 6–7.5; 75–81°F (24–27°C). In tank, provide partially sandy bottom with fairly sparse vegetation. Keep at least eight fishes. Feed with frozen Saldula variabilis, food pellets (broken into tiny pieces), and small worm food. **Socialization** With three *Otocinclus* catfishes in 6 gallons (25 L) of water; in 9 gallons (35 L) additionally with seven Redfin Pencilfishes or twelve Ember Tetras. **Similar** *Corydoras pygmaeus*, 1.2 inches (3 cm); *Corydoras hastatus*, 1.5 inches (3.5 cm); *Aspidoras pauciradiatus*, 1.2 inches (3 cm).

West African Nano

Most West African nanofishes come from cool, shady rain forest streams with mainly sandy bottoms and accumulations of dead wood. Aquatic plants are fairly uncommon.

Species Dwarf Barbs and Killifishes predominate. Killifishes are usually very colorful and are found in the tiniest ankle-deep rivulets. It seems that they are naturally adapted to conditions in a nano. Thus, in this exceptional case the Cape Lopez Lyretail, which grows up to 2.4 inches (6 cm), can be kept with a clear conscience in a 3-gallon (12-L) tank.

Setup Since there is little thick aquatic vegetation in West Africa, but rather beautiful epiphyte plants from the genus *Anubias*, a setup kept dark with a red-brown sandy bottom and roots as well as tied-on epiphyte plants is appropriate. The shimmering colors, which make the killifishes in particular so charming, occur only in conditions of low lighting. These fishes tolerate *Anubias* and Java Moss almost exclusively. In tanks with too much light, these fishes remain pale and shy.

Stocking In fairly large tanks of at least 9 gallons (35 L). Dwarf Barbs and Killis get along well, but in smaller nanos up to 6 gallons (25 L). there is not enough space. This calls for just one species or the other. African Dwarf Barbs are sociable schooling fishes that must be kept in a bunch. They like to root around in the soft substrate. With Killifishes and others such as the Cape Lopez Lyretail, if you want to breed fishes, you should keep just one species.

Particulars Most Killis regularly spawn near the surface of the water in Java Moss. The eggs can be collected by hand, for they have very hard shells. They are transferred to a separate small dish. An anti-fungal preparation from a pet shop is added to the water according to the directions, and the dish is suspended in the tank or in a hanging basket. The larvae hatch after about two weeks. Two to three days in advance the water in the dish needs to be replaced with water from the tank. The fry are transferred in the suspended baskets and are fed drop by drop with "Liquifry for Live Bearers" (available in pet shops); after about a week they can be fed *Artemia* nauplii.

Epiplatys annulatus
Clown Killie

1.2 inches (3.5 cm). **Origin** Insectivorous surface fish in West African swampy waters containing lots of vegetation. **Care** Soft to medium-hard, slightly acidic water (pH 6–7); 70–77°F (21–25°C). Provide thick vegetation and a cover of aquatic plants. Keep one male with two to three females. Eats dried food and small live food. Females spawn on aquatic plants. Larvae are raised with paramecia in suspended boxes. **Socialization** In 9 gallons (35 L) with eight Dwarf Barbs or six to eight small, bottom-dwelling fishes. **Similar** *Fenerbahce formosus*, 1.2 inches (3 cm); *Aphyoplatys duboisi*, 1.4 inches (3.5 cm).

Barbus jae
Jae Barb

1.2 inches (3 cm). **Origin** The tiniest clear-water streams in Central Africa's rain forest. **Care** The lively Barbs are suited only for nanos of 6 gallons (25 L) or larger; soft, slightly acidic water (pH 5.5–6.5); 72–75°F (22–24°C). Set up the tank with partially sandy substrate, roots, and epiphyte plants. Keep at least eight fishes. Feed with small frozen and live food, e.g., *Saldula variabilis,* grindal worms. Difficult to breed. **Socialization** In 9 gallons (35 L) with surface fishes, e.g., three Clown Killies or three Cape Lopez Lyretails. **Similar** Butterfly Barb (*Barbus hulstaerti*), 1.5 inches (3.5 cm).

Aphyosemion australe
Cape Lopez Lyretail

2.3 inches (6 cm). **Origin** Insectivores in the tiniest rain forest streams of Gabon's coastal marshes. **Care** Soft to medium-hard, slightly acidic water (pH 5–6.5); 72–75°F (22–24°C). Thick vegetation here and there, small roots for hiding places. In a 3-gallon (12-L) nano, keep one male with two or three females. Feed with small insects, fine frozen and live food, and dried food if necessary. Eggs are spawned onto plants and can be incubated in suspended boxes. **Socialization** In 6-gallon (25-L) tank with eight Dwarf Barbs. **Similar** *Aphyosemion elberti*, 2 inches (5 cm); *A. exiguum*, 1.6 inches (4 cm).

Asian Nano

The typical habitats of Asian small fish species are found in small bodies of water located in swampy peat forests. They always channel black water and are characterized by thick layers of fallen leaves. The fishes are also often found in less open landscapes, with clear or cloudy water with weedy plant growth. Sometimes the creatures also live in flooded rice fields.

Species The character types of these waters include the most popular nano fishes: the Dwarf Barbs of the genera *Boraras* and *Danio*, the Scarlet Badis of the genus *Dario*, and Labyrinth fishes of the genera *Trichopsis*, *Betta,* and *Parosphromenus*. Labyrinth fishes are decidedly reserved, but Danionins and Scarlet Badis are quite lively.

Setup The habitat types mentioned above hardly lead to a common denominator with respect to water quality and setup. Blackwater tanks should be filtered through peat and should contain nearly no carbonate hardness. They can be planted only with a few acid-resistant plant species, such as Java Moss and Humped Bladderwort. The setup should offer a thin layer of sand, small roots, and a few autumn beech leaves plucked from trees. "Weed tanks," on the other hand, are planted thick with *Cryptocoryne*, Java Moss, Java Fern, and the little Water Wisteria. A layer of floating aquatic plants provides cover.

Stocking The rather lively Danionins are suited to fairly large nanos of 9 gallons (35 L) or larger as company for *Dario* species and small labyrinth fishes. The latter are kept in pairs.

Particulars The smallest freshwater fishes in the world, the *Paedocypris* species, also come from the blackwater regions of Southeast Asia. They grow to be hardly ⅜ inch (1 cm) long. They can thus be kept in a nanotank, but they rarely reproduce in a tank.

The beloved labyrinth fishes, e.g., the Sparkling or Pygmy Gouramis, are distinguished by a particular ability. Through the so-called labyrinth, a deeply folded breathing organ in the area behind the head, they extract oxygen from atmospheric air on the surface of the water.

Boraras maculatus
Dwarf Rasbora

1 inch (2.5 cm). **Origin** Areas of fallen plants and leaves along the banks of slow-flowing or stagnant water in Malaysia. **Care** Soft to medium-hard, acidic water (pH 5–6.5); peat filtering; 72–79°F (22–26° C). Plants including fine, feathery species and a layer of aquatic plants. For schooling fishes, keep at least twelve. Feed with small live food, or dry food from time to time. **Socialization** In 9 gallons (35 L) with a couple of Darios or Pygmy Gouramies. **Similar** Redfin Dwarf Rasbora (*B. brigittae*), blackwater fish, ¾ inch (2 cm); Least Rasbora (*B. urophthalmoides*), 0.6 inch (1.6 cm).

Dario dario
Bengal Dario

1.2 inches (3 cm). **Origin** Weedy streams in northern India. **Care** Soft to medium-hard water, pH 6.5–7.5; 68–79°F (20–26°C). Thick plant growth and decorations including one or two waterlogged beech leaves. Relatively undemanding species; keep one male with two or three females. Feed with small live and frozen food, e.g., *Saldula variabilis* and *Artemia* nauplii. The fishes spawn in Java Moss; hatchlings grow up on their own. Their first food is microorganisms present in the nano. **Socialization** In 9 gallons (35 L) with twelve Dwarf Barbs. **Similar** *Dario hysginon*, 1.4 inches (3.5 cm).

Trichopsis pumila
Sparkling or Pygmy Gourami

1.6 inches (4 cm). **Origin** Weedy still waters. **Care** pH over 5.5; 73–81°F (23–27°C). Can also be kept in pairs in the smallest, thickly planted nanos of at least 3 gallons (12 L). Feed with fine living or dry food. The male establishes a territory and emits audible noises (purring). Builds a foam nest under broad-leafed aquatic plants and cares for the eggs. Feed larvae four days after hatching with *Artemia* nauplii; after two weeks with grindal worms. **Socialization** In 9 gallons (35 L) with twelve Dwarf Barbs.

Crustacean Tanks

The boom in nanoaquariums initially had something to do with the small shrimps, which were becoming increasingly popular. For this reason nanos are often bought as "shrimp aquariums."

Species Asian Dwarf Shrimps from the genus *Caridina* and *Neocaridina* are among the most attractive and beloved nano creatures. There are even breeding forms of Bee Shrimps, for which four-figure dollar amounts are paid in many places. In addition to shrimps, the mini-crabs from the genus *Cambarellus* are very popular.

Setup Most dwarf shrimps live in streams, where they gather tiny particles of food with busy scissors movements in fallen leaves or among the roots and leaves of land plants. Dwarf river crabs, on the other hand, prefer rather weedy still water. A requirement for keeping all species of shrimp in a nanoaquarium is a well-broken-in tank in which abundant microorganisms and decaying plant matter, such as brown autumn leaves from beeches or oaks, are available. Air-driven foam filters and Hamburg mat filters (see page 11), which produce no strong current, are preferable to other filters, for the shrimps can use the upper surface of the filter as an eating place and gather microorganisms there. The set-up should include fine-grained substrate, roots with Java Moss, and a few autumn leaves.

Stocking Most species should not be kept too warm, and this reason alone they are not well suited for being placed with most freshwater aquarium fishes. One exception is the *Otocinclus* catfish, which can be kept with the shrimps in a 6-gallon (25-L) nano. Dwarf shrimps must be kept in a fairly large group of at least ten. In contrast, Dwarf River Shrimps are kept in pairs or alone.

Particulars Many species of crustaceans reproduce naturally in an aquarium. The females carry an egg packet under their abdomen, and after a certain time living larvae develop from it. They can remain in the tank with the parents.

Cambarellus patzcuarensis
Orange Dwarf Crayfish

1.6 inches (4 cm). **Origin** Weedy shores of standing waters in Mexico. **Care** At least a 6-gallon (25-L) aquarium; water medium-hard to hard, in no case acidic (pH 7–8); unheated tank; temperatures of 61–77°F (16–25°C). No strong filtration so that there is always some decayed material or remains of fallen leaves available as a nutritional supplement to dried plant food. Keep animals in pairs. **Socialization** Should be avoided, for Dwarf Crays are otherwise too reserved to come to the food provided. **Similar** Other *Cambarellus* species.

Caridina cf. *cantonensis*
Bee Shrimp, Crystal Red Shrimp

0.8 inch (2 cm). **Origin** "Crystal Red" is a breeding form of the Bee shrimp from South China. **Care** Soft to medium-hard water, pH 6.5–7.5; winter temperatures of 50–59°F (10–15°C) encourage reproduction; in Summer, 73–86°F (23–30°C). Keep at least twelve to twenty shrimps. Feed with rabbit pellets and dry shrimp food. Breeding: fertilized females carry the eggs for four weeks until developed larvae are released. **Socialization** In 9 gallons (35 L) with three *Otocinclus* catfishes. **Similar** Red-fire Shrimp (*Neocardina* cf. *heteropoda*), 1.2 inches (3 cm).

Caridina cf. *babaulti* "green"
Green Neon Shrimp

0.8 inch (2 cm). **Origin** A broad variety of water types in Asian lowlands from Myanmar to North India. **Care** Soft to medium-hard water, pH 6.5–7; likes higher temperatures from 75–79°F (24–26°C). Tank must be well broken-in and planted thickly. Calm, sociable shrimps, of which at least fifteen should be kept. Feed occasionally with rabbit pellets and tiny amounts of dry food. **Socialization** In 9 gallons (35 L) with three Otocinclus crayfishes. **Similar** Malaya Shrimp (*Caridina* cf. *babaulti* "Malaya").

Jewels for a Nanotank

Here, we introduce some of the most beautiful species that are kept and bred. Many of them are available only on special order at pet shops or through special interest groups.

CELESTIAL PEARL DANIO *(Danio margaritatus)* These fishes are extremely beautiful, gregarious, and undemanding. They require thick vegetation.

PAROSPHROMENUS GOURAMIES Courting males of this genus from Southeast Asia (here, *Parosphromenus nagyi*) are among the most attractive freshwater fishes. They need very soft and acidic water and tiny live food.

REDFIN DWARF RASBORA or **MOSQUITO RASBORA** *(Boraras brigittae)* This species comes from blackwater swamps in Borneo, where it lives with other dwarf fishes. This schooling fish requires low pH and hardness levels.

NEOLEBIAS POWELLI This dwarf Tetra lives in black water in the Niger Delta in Nigeria. It needs dim lighting and soft water.

GABON JEWEL FISH *(Diapteron cyanostictum)* Keep one male and two females of this killifish from Gabon. The nano should have soft water.

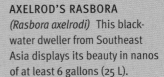

AXELROD'S RASBORA *(Rasbora axelrodi)* This black-water dweller from Southeast Asia displays its beauty in nanos of at least 6 gallons (25 L).

BUTTERFLY BARB *(Barbus hulstaerti)* This schooling fish from the Congo loves to swim, so it is appropriate for nanos of at least 6 gallons (25 L). Don't keep too warm—preferably around 72°F (22°C).

MATANO CARDINAL SHRIMP *(Neocaridina sp.)* This shrimp lives under rocks in the crystal-clear Lake Matano on the island of Sulawesi. Little is known about the care requirements of this species.

Purchase, Care, and Breeding

The aquarium is set up and planted, and the break-in phase is complete. At last fishes and crustaceans can take up residence in the nano. In the following pages you will learn what you have to look for, how daily care is handled, and even how to produce young.

The Most Important Tips for Purchasing

Ideally, you have gathered information beforehand on where you can get the desired fishes or crustaceans. Of course, it is important to get healthy creatures, so it's best to go to a reliable pet shop. Local aquarium clubs or experienced aquarium hobbyists can give you helpful tips.

A good pet shop owner will spend time with you and ask questions about your aquarium. If you are interested in unusual species that are rather difficult to get, you will also get support from the specialty trade, for the retailers can ask for specific fishes from a variety of suppliers.

There are also many aquarium animals that are available on the market only sporadically. In this case it is useful to approach specialty clubs, which can help in many ways (see Resources, page 62).

Recognizing Healthy Animals

Before you decide on what you will purchase, you should take a careful look at the vitality of your future aquarium inhabitants. Many diseases can be identified through unmistakable symptoms, but unfortunately others cannot—at least not in the beginning stages. Be sure to observe the selected creatures for a while.

› Do they eat normally? If necessary, have the creatures demonstrate that they are eating properly.
› Are they active in accordance with their age and species?
› Do they look like they have lost weight—with hollow belly and angular back ("knife back")?
› Are they in clear water, or is there perhaps a bluish, yellowish, or greenish tint to the water from medications in the dealer's tank?

Note: Never buy any fishes from tanks with creatures that appear to be sick.

Transporting the Fishes Home and Putting Them in the Tank

Fishes and shrimps are transported in plastic bags that are filled a third of their capacity with water and two thirds with air. In cold weather, place the bag in a Styrofoam container or wrap it in a thick layer of newspaper. As soon as you get home with your new creatures, place them into their new home with as little stress as possible. Here's how to do it.

The Right Temperature First place the unopened bag on the surface of the water in the aquarium and leave it for about a half hour to reach the right temperature.

Acclimation In order for the fishes to get used to the new chemical composition of the water, open the bag after the half hour and carefully add about a quarter of the amount of water that is in the bag from the aquarium. Repeat this process twice in intervals of about fifteen minutes.

Putting Them In Now the temperature and water values are in balance. Carefully use a net to remove the creatures from the transport bag and transfer them to their new home.

Overcoming Initial Problems

Once the creatures are successfully placed in the aquarium, the following problems may sometimes arise in the tank.

Detectable Nitrite After putting the fishes in the tank, nitrite values are often detectable with drop tests (see page 9), even though the values were below the suggested limits after the break-in phase and before putting in the fishes. The cause for the sudden presence of the poisonous nitrite is that the filter bacteria evidently were not developed to the necessary quantity, or that there are too many fishes. You can help by changing three quarters of the aquarium water and repeating this process once a day until the measured levels are perfect.

The adult males of the Bengal *Dario* show their beautiful coloration only some time after being put into the tank.

To equalize the temperature, the transfer bag with the fishes inside is placed on the surface of the water in the tank for around a half hour.

A fine-mesh net is used to take the fishes out of the transfer bag and release them into the aquarium so that no water from the bag gets into the tank.

Cloudiness A milky cloudiness in the tank is normal after a new setup or cleaning activity. It disappears spontaneously in no more than a couple of days. Don't do anything if you notice this cloudiness.

String Algae If you use substrate fertilizers when you set up your aquarium, there can be a massive growth of long, threadlike string algae. These should be wound around a small stick and removed regularly.

Smear Algae A few days after initial setup, a musty smelling, dark green "carpet of algae" may develop on the substrate, accessories, and plants. This is easy to remove, but it grows back after a few days and covers everything once again. The cause of this algae is bacteria that are known as blue–green, cyanophyta, smear, or slime algae. Unfortunately there is no remedy for this, for the precise reason for its appearance is not known. Smear algae evidently like unstable conditions, for they are present when the tank is not yet properly

broken in. However, they also appear when the tank is unstable for other reasons. It's best to remove the mats of bacteria as completely as possible and keep sucking them up with a hose for weeks (see page 50). If possible, the aquarium should simultaneously be kept dark for several days. Using peat filtration or putting in tropical almond tree leaves often helps.

Effective **Medicinal Plants**

The leaves of the widely distributed tropical almond tree *Terminalia catappa* are not only decorative—they also give off substances that combat bacteria. Therefore it never hurts to put a tropical almond tree leaf into the transfer bag and aquarium water. Blackwater fishes in particular appreciate this addition.

An Overview of Feeding

In the wild, there is a tremendous variety of food available to creatures that can be kept in a nano tank. This includes plankton such as little crustaceans and their larvae, tiny insects that fall into the water, insect larvae, small worms, and even pollen. In addition, decaying plant leaves and nutrient-rich mud are consumed. Since they are accustomed to this natural variety, the creatures also need a varied diet in an aquarium.

Many species like food pellets, but it is hard to administer the right amount of this type of food.

Dry Food

Dry food is also used by experienced aquarium hobbyists, because it is easy to get and it supplies the most important basic needs of many fishes. The requirements of most nano dwellers are met adequately with high-quality flake food or fine pellets, preferably in combination with frozen and live food. Whether a particular type is suited for a specific fish species depends on the form in which it is offered and its content of high-quality ingredients.

Various Forms Dry food comes in the form of flakes, granules, pellets, and powder. Open water fishes like to eat fine pellet and flake food, and pellets are a good choice for catfishes. High-quality food contains fiber and lots of natural red ingredients that are also present in many crustaceans (color-enhancing food). It also has a percentage of spirulina algae, which contains many important nutrients. There is a special dry food for shrimps.

Keeping Small Quantities on Hand Since nano creatures use very little food, most commonly available food containers contain excessively large quantities. The food loses its quality before it is used; therefore it is best to divide it up and freeze it so that only small quantities are opened. Store the thawed dry food in an opaque container in the refrigerator.

Frozen Food

Frozen food animals certainly don't move, but they retain the same important ingredients as live food animals—provided that the frozen food is of high quality. As long as they are kept properly, food animals that are caught outdoors are superior in nutrients to many types of dry food, and even to food animals that have been bred or kept in storage for a long time. In addition, there is a wide variety of frozen food animals.

The Most Important Types of Frozen Foods for Nanocreatures These include various small crustaceans, which make up the majority of the plankton in stagnant waters. Because of their high carotenoid content (natural red pigments) they are particularly valuable. Mosquito larvae are another favorite food.

› Water fleas, including "normal" water fleas (*Daphnia*), *Moina* water fleas, and *Bosmina* water fleas are part of the standard selection. *Daphnia* are rich in fiber and are therefore an ideal complement to other types of foods. However, feeding with *Daphnia* alone can lead to deficiency symptoms.

› *Cyclops* and *Diaptomus* water fleas are smaller than many water flea species are but richer in nutrients. A balanced diet is possible for many small fish species with only *Cyclops*, but like all single-food diets, it's not the best option.

› *Artemia* nauplii are the larval stage of the saltwater crustacean *Artemia*, which can be incubated from eggs (see page 48). We also strongly recommend them as frozen food.

› Black, red, and white mosquito larvae are too large for most nanofishes, but they can be cut up.

Seven **Golden Rules for Feeding**

DRY AND FROZEN FOOD	Feed rather small amounts, as much as a creature can eat in two to three minutes. Leftover food contaminates the water and must be removed.	**QUALITY**	Use only high-quality types of foods containing valuable ingredients, such as *Spirulina* algae.
LIVE FOOD	Live food can be given in slightly larger amounts, for the creatures will continue to live in the aquarium. *Artemia* nauplii are one exception; since they occur naturally in saltwater, they die in freshwater.	**VARIETY**	Combining several types of foods and including live food covers the nutritional needs better than using a single type of food.
		TYPICAL REQUIREMENTS	Observe the lifestyles of the individual species: bottom-dwelling fishes don't eat at the surface, and vice-versa; nocturnal species generally don't eat during the day.
FROZEN FOOD	Upon purchase, make sure the food has not been thawed. Ideally it should be thawed immediately before feeding and rinsed in a strainer to keep from contaminating the tank water with tiny particles from the thaw water.	**AMOUNT**	Feeding a little bit several times a day is better than feeding a lot all at once; this applies especially to young fishes. One day of fasting per week is also beneficial.

Black mosquito larvae in particular provide optimal nutrients.

Note: Some people are extremely allergic to red mosquito larvae, which are sold as bloodworms. These are not the larvae of the true mosquito, but are a good food source nonetheless. If you suspect an allergic reaction, be sure to consult a doctor.

Live Food

Even if dry and frozen food provide all necessary nutrients, it still makes sense to provide live food, and it is even vitally important for some fishes. They need live food, for it takes the movements of the food animals to trigger the stimulus to eat.

1 *Artemia* nauplii: After feeding the nauplii, the culture dish must be cleaned with warm water and a brush. This keeps a film from forming on it.

2 Grindal worms: You should renew the culture every three months. Always keep several in operation, for not all cultures thrive.

This applies to such nanoinhabitants as certain Gobies, Scarlet Badises, some killifishes, and Gouramies.

Sources of Live Food There are several possible sources of live food.

> Sometimes there is a good assortment in pet shops, but it varies according to season. Usually the food animals are too large for the tiny nano dwellers.
> The best option is to catch the food animals yourself, but this works only if you have the appropriate materials, that is, a net with a fine mesh, suitable ponds, and any necessary permission to collect food animals. This possibility is not available to everyone. In addition, the captured food animals must be sorted by size and stored in aerated containers. You can find information on the Internet concerning the construction or purchase of nets and strainers.
> Breeding water fleas and mosquito larvae in rain barrels is possible only for property owners, and can be done only during the warm seasons.

Breeding *Artemia* nauplii

One ideal option for obtaining high-quality live food is to breed *Artemia* nauplii. The larvae of the salt water crustacean, which can be hatched easily from eggs, provide fishes with a valuable source of nutrients, and normally they are typically always available.

Obtaining Eggs Eggs are available in pet shops in various amounts and qualities. If you don't have young fishes to feed you can get larger eggs, but you should note the freshness date on the packaging. A fairly large number of eggs can be purchased to provide a supply; divide them up into airtight, sealable baggies (volume of about 2 ounces) and freeze them. This will allow the eggs to last for over a year. The right amount of eggs for each feeding is removed, and the bag is closed and stored in the refrigerator.

Hatching *Artemia* Nauplii If you need only a fairly small amount of nauplii, the special hatching dishes are adequate (see illustration on facing page); they are placed in a warm location (72–82°F/22–28°C). They are filled with saltwater (1 ounce/30 g of iodine-free table salt or sea salt per quart of water), and about a pinch of artemia eggs for every ten fishes to be fed are placed into the saltwater. After around 24 to 36 hours (the warmer, the shorter the wait), the reddish nauplii hatch.

Feeding Nauplii The nauplii are separated from the eggshells by shining a light on the underside of the incubation container, which is designed for this purpose. The light-seeking nauplii collect there and can be sucked up from the bottom with a pipette or a plastic syringe. They are placed into an *Artemia* strainer from the pet shop, rinsed under tap water, and placed directly into the tank with a teaspoon. Make sure that no eggshells are put in, for they will contaminate the water and are not tolerated by many fishes.

Hatching Larger Amounts If you have several nanos or need lots of nauplii, it's better to use special *Artemia* culture devices from a pet shop. These are aerated bottles in which larger amounts of eggs can be hatched, for example, for raising young fishes, so that the nauplii don't have to suffer from a lack of oxygen because of the high concentration.

Important Always keep two dishes or culture devices going and replace one every 24 hours with a new one so that you always have enough *Artemia* nauplii available. Occasionally clean the dishes with hot water.

Raising **Grindal Worms**

A TIP FROM THE EXPERT:
Ulrich Schliewen

The very nutritious grindal worms are a good supplementary food for bottom-dwelling nanospecies. However, they contain too much fat to be used as a single food source. Here's how to raise the worms:

STEP ONE   Prepare a piece of foam in a cross shape with an empty space in the middle for the food. Put the foam into a plastic container measuring about 4 × 6 inches (10 × 15 cm), such as in a refrigerator container with a gauze covering to allow air circulation.

STEP TWO   Place 1 teaspoon of powdered baby cereal, very soft oatmeal, or cooked oatmeal into the empty area as worm food and moisten it; the starter should not be in the water.

STEP THREE   Add the worm starter (available through aquarium magazines or on the Internet), and place a small plate of glass on it (around 3½ inches/8 cm in diameter).

STEP FOUR   Put the culture into a warm, dark place. After a few days there will be worms under the cover; you can remove them with a small brush and feed them directly to the fishes.

Taking Care of a Nano

A nanotank requires limited care. However, you should thoroughly inspect the aquarium every day, for a nano reacts much more sensitively to errors in caregiving than a larger tank does because of the small volume of water.

The Daily Nano Check

The most important tasks are daily observation, feeding, and counting of all aquarium inhabitants. Take time with the feeding and try to observe every fish. Watch for changes in behavior or appearance and check that all fishes show up for feeding. If one inhabitant—even a fairly large snail—comes up missing, you must search for and remove the dead creature so that the aquarium water doesn't become contaminated.

If you identify problems early, you can deal with them, such as treating illnesses or separating fishes that don't get along together. Of course it is just as important to check out the mechanical devices every day: Is the filter working? Is the water temperature right?

Weekly Care

Partial Water Change No aquarium can do without partial water changes in intervals of one to two weeks. This involves exchanging around 20 percent of the water, for even with optimal care contaminants build up and cannot be broken down by the filter bacteria or absorbed by the plants.

A water change in a nano is not a major task. All you need is a small hose and two watering cans with no more than 2½ gallons (10 L) of water. If you use special water (see page 16), you also need to have a supply of prepared water on hand.

Before doing the water change, turn off all mechanical devices to avoid running the pump and heater while dry. Then let about a fifth of the aquarium water run through the hose and into the watering can.

At the same time suck up leftover food and decayed material from the bottom. Then finish by putting the prepared water into the tank.

Cleaning the Glass In addition to the substrate, plants, and decorations, the aquarium glass also gets covered with bacteria and algae with time. Even though some algae growth is desirable, it is an interference on the front pane and is

A watering can makes it very easy to perform a partial water change in a nanotank.

difficult to remove if it proliferates there too long. The easiest way to avoid this is by using an algae sponge or a magnet window cleaner. Clean the front glass once a week, even if you can't see any algae growth. This will avoid a stubborn algae infestation.

Care in Longer Intervals

Cleaning the Filter A biological filter is the heart of every aquarium, and it requires serious care. However, too much care is just as harmful as too little, so between partial water changes, wash only the first coarse filter layer (not always present, depending on type of filter) under lukewarm water until the rinse water remains clear.

The following filter layers are good for a longer time, because the first layer catches the coarse dirt. For the other layers it is more advantageous to not disturb their bacteria cultures at all. These layers should be rinsed only if there are signs that they are becoming clogged by filtered material.

To avoid disturbing the bacteria, don't use hot water. Chemical–physical filter materials cannot be regenerated by washing. Thus, peat and active carbon, for example, must be regularly replaced if the desired filtration effect has not yet been reached.

Maintaining and Calibrating Mechanical Devices Some components of pumps, filters, and lighting get dirty and wear out with time, so they must be replaced or adjusted.

> Small motor pumps: Drive wheels and pump axles easily get dirty and wear out; this is detectable through a slight chattering noise. The parts must be cleaned according to their instructions or must be replaced. Sometimes even tiny snails get inside and need to be removed.

> Membrane pumps: After a year or two the rubber membranes wear out. Be sure to replace them.

> Lighting: Light bulbs wear out with time even though they continue to give off light, and the change is usually not noticeable. But this can have a negative effect on plant care, for there are changes in the intensity and composition of the light spectrum. Fluorescent tubes should be changed at yearly intervals.

> Consumable materials: Consumables from carbon dioxide fertilizing devices and automatic fluid fertilizers need to be refilled.

2 A dip tube keeps too much gravel or sand from being sucked up while vacuuming the substrate. It's better to use a fairly small hose.

1 A rough algae sponge from a pet store is the best tool for removing algae growth from aquarium glass.

Plant Care

To make the aquatic plants in the aquarium last a long time, they need special care and attention.

Make sure your plants get an adequate supply of the right nutrients and appropriate aquarium water.

Plants also need light for photosynthesis and must be protected from algae that would otherwise grow wild on them. Often the plants thrive at first, but after a few months the growth stagnates and algae takes over the plants.

Providing Plants with Nutrients

Nutrient Fertilizers Plants get their nutrition from dissolved substances in the water and substrate. About once a month, or more frequently under conditions of bright light, they need the addition of liquid fertilizer for aquarium plants. Place this into the water according to the directions. Fertilizers for potted plants are not suitable, for they encourage excessive algae growth. Two types of fertilizer are used, a general one and an iron

A richly planted tank not only looks attractive but also provides a structured environment. To keep the nano from getting overgrown, the plants must be regularly thinned out and cut back.

fertilizer. The latter is always necessary when the plants stop growing and produce yellow leaves instead of green ones. Rooting plants are fertilized monthly with pieces of special fertilizer pellets for aquatic plants; these are placed into the substrate in the vicinity of the roots.

Carbon Dioxide (CO_2) The most important plant nutrients are provided through strong lighting, significant fertilizing, and thick planting. There are more or less automated devices for nanotanks that provide a continuous supply of CO_2. The important thing is to fertilize with CO_2 only during the day, because plants cannot process it in the dark. If you fertilize with CO_2 you need to be familiar with the connection between carbonate hardness, CO_2 content, and pH (see page 15).

Keeping the Plants Healthy

To keep a nanotank from becoming overgrown in the twinkling of an eye, the plants must also be kept within bounds by regularly thinning them out or cutting them back. Here's how it's done:

> Stem plants: If they become too long and leafless below, pull them out of the substrate, trim them at the bottom with scissors, and put the top part back in as top cuttings.

> Rosette plants: Superfluous runners in the substrate should be carefully separated with your fingers or a pair of scissors, and should then be removed.

Aerating the Substrate

Aquarium plants need a breathing substrate with a good oxygen supply for the roots. This is achieved by loosening up the substrate with a stick every couple of weeks, or by placing trumpet snails in the substrate. These creatures burrow through the substrate and aerate it.

In fairly large tanks, *Otocinclus* catfishes are good for controlling algae, which they continually scrape away.

Keeping Algae Within Bounds

Algae growth is a problem, especially on slow-growing aquarium plants, and it often is hard to get under control. Many creatures eat algae, which can be helpful. However, there are only a few that are appropriate for the dwarf species in nanotanks. Particularly good choices are Ottos (*Otocinclus* catfishes), which are put in from the beginning in a small group of around three to five creatures. Many shrimp species also handle algae well. Whichever species you choose, make sure that they get enough green matter once the algae are sufficiently cleaned up. Most species accept substitutes in the form of small pieces of zucchini, which must be replaced daily.

Caring for Your Nano During Vacation

In contrast to fish species in aquariums of normal size, the dwarf fishes in a nano have hardly any nutritional reserves, so they are not in a position to withstand days of hunger without harm. However, you can leave with a clear conscience as long as you take a few measures beforehand.

Short Vacation An absence of a few days is the easiest to get through. Before the start of a vacation, healthy adult fishes are given the requisite amount of live food that will last for several days and will tolerate fresh water (no *Artemia*). Adult nanocreatures can even make it through one or two days without any food at all. Therefore, it is not a problem to leave the aquarium for a short while without further preparation, provided that the mechanical accessories are working flawlessly and it has not been too long since the last water change.

Longer Absences

If you are planning a longer vacation, here is one important ground rule: Except for a partial water change, make no changes shortly before the start of the trip. Don't put in any new devices or inhabitants, for you can no longer determine if the new changes have any harmful effects.

Getting a Replacement For longer absences you should ask a person you trust to feed the creatures regularly, check the mechanical devices, and perform partial water changes. If this person is not experienced with aquariums, you must carefully instruct him or her for several days until all chores have been covered. If you have a single nano tank, you can also proceed as follows: Let out two-thirds of the water and bring the whole tank and its contents in this condition to the vacation caregiver.

Automatic dispensers for dry food are helpful in providing food during short absences. However, only very small amounts must be dispensed to keep from contaminating the water.

The Best Care for a Nano

A couple of simple rules help turn a nanoaquarium with a capacity of only a few quarts into an aesthetically superior and appropriate environment.

Good Practices

Things to Avoid

+ Learn as much as you can about the requirements of your nano—your knowledge will have a good effect on the best way to set up the miniature environment.

+ Always keep 10 to 20 quarts of appropriate water on hand for a partial water change. In many cases, problems can be solved in a matter of minutes with a partial water change.

+ Frequently provide live food, for it keeps longer and doesn't contaminate the water as much as dry food.

+ Always dispense food and medications in exact amounts. In so doing, always consider the net water content of the nano tank.

− Never put in more than one—or in fairly large nanos of at least 6 gallons (25 L), two—species of fish or shrimp.

− Don't use any water-care products that promise to drastically raise the water quality in the aquarium without providing precise information on the ingredients. No product can take the place of thorough care.

− Don't fiddle around with the aquarium needlessly. A nano reacts like a small organism that adjusts with difficulty to changes in conditions.

− Don't raise young creatures in the nano until they are big, but rather in a tank of their own. As they grow they could burst the tank's contamination limits in a very short time.

Diseases and Pests

If water care, socialization, tank setup, and feeding are handled properly, diseases will rarely occur. But since there are many bacteria present in every aquarium, a weakening of the immune system can lead to infections. The creatures become susceptible to disease if they are not kept under appropriate living conditions or if they are still stressed out from transport.

Preventive Measures Observing the creatures every day, checking the water temperature, performing regular partial water changes, and providing a varied diet are the best preventive measures. Smear algae should be fixed early on before it has a harmful impact on the water (see page 45), and even the population of snails should be kept small.

White spot disease is the most common fish disease. This photo shows a sick Three Spot Gourami, which is not a nanospecies.

The Most Common Diseases

"White Spot Disease" or "Ich" If a fish is covered with individual white dots up to 0.05 inch/ 1.5 mm in size, frequently rubs up against things, and breathes more quickly than normal, it probably has become infected with the one-celled *Ichthyophthirius*. Pet shops offer a wide variety of effective medications. Be sure to follow carefully the treatment times provided in the directions, plus the use in the aquarium itself, since the resting forms can lead to the reappearance of infections. Raise the temperature to 82°F (28°C) to complement the treatment. Unfortunately, a very resistant form of this disease appeared a few years ago. If a normal treatment does not work, consult an expert.

"Gold Dust Disease" or Oodinium This disease is first detectible on the fins, and later on the entire body, as a fine white or golden "layer of dust." Like White Spot disease, the fishes with this disease rub against things. The cause is an infestation with the single-celled organism *Oodinium*, which can be tackled in medium-hard to hard water with special medications from the pet shop. In soft-water tanks, the infection is treated with additions of common salt (2 to a maximum of 4 teaspoons of salt containing no iodine or additives per 10 quarts of water). If the disease abates, perform several partial water changes to keep from stressing the fishes and plants. In addition, all snails should be removed, for they are often the intermediate hosts. *Costia*, another single-celled pathogen, can also be responsible for similar symptoms. It can be effectively combated with medications that contain malachite green oxalate.

Additional Diseases There are many other fish diseases, which you can find out about in scientific literature, from a specialized veterinarian (ads in aquarium periodicals), or from aquarium clubs.

Be Careful When Giving Medications

In dispensing medications in a nano, you have to use extreme caution because of the small volume of water. In other words, calculate the doses precisely based on the net water volume and measure the amounts of medications with a dosage syringe or a postage scale.

One drop corresponds to about 0.3 mg. If necessary, dilute the medication in a ratio of 1:10 with distilled water and calculate the dosage to produce a larger volume to keep on hand.

Other Pests in a Nanotank

In addition to snails and algae, planaria and hydra are harmful in a nano. These pests are introduced on plants or live food, and sometimes they reproduce quickly.

Planaria (flatworms) are wormlike creatures that are easy to identify on the glass of the aquarium, and crawl like tiny, flat slugs. They are difficult to combat but two methods have proven successful.

It is best to empty out the aquarium entirely and disinfect both the tank and the accessories with appropriate products that can be obtained from a pet store.

During this time, the aquarium inhabitants are kept in a bucket with aquarium water at the proper temperature while giving the plants an alum bath.

A second method is to remove the fishes and shrimps, raise the temperature to 90°F (32°C) for

Freshwater polyps are small, stinging creatures that sometimes get introduced with live food from the outdoors. They can harm young fishes.

three days, and repeat the whole process after seven days to kill the eggs as well.

Hydra (freshwater polyps), like jelly fishes, are stinging coelenterates on a miniature scale that particularly thrive when live food is provided. The mostly green or yellowish creatures lodge on plants and panes of glass. With their stinging tentacles, they can be dangerous to very small and young fishes. To counteract them, they can be starved by providing no live food for the tank inhabitants for a month. However, a resurgence of the *Hydra* epidemic is easily possible.

You can also kill *Hydra* with ammonium appropriate products available at a pet store. Be sure to then perform a repeated partial water change. If you have no shrimps, you can also place a small piece of copper or brass tubing into the tank for two weeks. Crustaceans will not survive this.

Successful Breeding in a Nanoaquarium

Even in a small nanotank many dwarf fishes and crustaceans find such a complete environment that they will reproduce. However, the eggs and larvae of most nanofishes and shrimps are so tiny and sensitive that you must give them the utmost care. In addition, the young creatures need special food. It's best to carefully transfer the eggs or larvae to one or more separate nursery containers so they don't get eaten by the other aquarium inhabitants, or even by their own parents.

A Suspended Cage

Small numbers of young fishes can be raised in suspended cages. A miniature air filter continually supplies them with tank water, which flows back into the tank (see illustration) through a fine-mesh screen (*Artemia* mesh from a pet shop). Depending on the species of fish, the eggs, larvae, or young fishes are carefully collected with a small plastic dish and transferred in such a way that they don't come into contact with the air. The young creatures tolerate the transfer well, for the temperature and the water values match those of the holding tank. They remain there until they are large enough to be transferred to a larger nursery tank. So-called "spawning boxes," which are available for isolating pregnant females of live-bearing fishes, are also available, but they are not suited as nursery containers for nanos, because the mesh is too large or they have fissures in them.

Nursery Tanks

Because of their greater need for water and space, larger amounts of young fishes must be raised in a nursery tank. This generally contains a heater, a large-volume sponge filter, and a device for intensive oxygen supply. In addition, it needs some objects to provide structure, such as floating plants and plastic tubes, beech leaves, branches, and roots.

This female Red Fire Shrimp carries yolk-yellow eggs that are visible beneath her abdomen.

Aerated suspended boxes help by separating the fry from their parents and making it possible to raise the tiny offspring with special food.

A wedge tank is also good for raising nanospecies. At first the fish larvae grow protected from the parents in the chamber on the right.

The fry (baby fishes) grow quickly when they are kept in water that is disturbed as little as possible and are provided with high-quality growth food at least twice a day. Depending on the population density, the required water quality is achieved through frequent partial water changes—every three to four days—with pre-prepared water. In addition, leftover food and droppings must be sucked up from the glass bottom.

Snails in the tank are useful in polishing off debris. Naturally, no sickly or misshapen fry must be raised.

Special Food for Fry

Many young fishes eat freshly hatched *Artemia* nauplii as their first food, which can be hatched in dishes (see page 48). Feed the fish larvae several times a day and suck up the dead *Artemia* with an air hose.

Many species also accept pulverized dry food as their first food, but we advise against this in a

nano, for it is difficult to dispense the right amount of food and the leftovers contaminate the water.

LiquiFry for egg layers (from a pet shop) has proven to be a good first food. Very small young fishes must be given extremely small live food in their first days until they are large enough to consume the *Artemia*. Single-celled paramecia are also an appropriate choice.

Raising Paramecia Fill a pint or quart (0.5–1 L) canning jar with water, put in one or two ½-inch (1-cm) pieces of dried banana peel, and add a culture starter from an active paramecium culture (available from aquarium clubs or online). Then wait a couple of days until the paramecia have reproduced, which is visible as a whitish cloud. Take out a few drops of this cloud with a pipette and dribble them straight into the nursery tank. The paramecium culture is fed with banana peel or four or five drops of condensed milk as soon as it clears up.

Pages numbers in **bold** print refer to illustrations.

Clubs/Societies

> Federation of American Aquarium Societies: *www.faas.into*. A directory of aquarium associations in the United States, Canada, and Latin America, that offers free membership and assistance in forming a new aquarium society.
> Canadian Association of Aquarium Clubs: *www.caoc.ca*. Contains links to twenty or more aquarium clubs in Canada.

Additional Literature

> Boruchowitz, David. *The Simple Guide to Freshwater Aquariums.* Neptune City, NJ: TFH Publications, 2001.

Important Note

> With electrical devices for aquariums, use only products that are designed and tested for their specific purpose.

> Regular water changes are essential for making your aquarium creatures feel their best.

> New water plants can cause poisoning. Always water and rinse to remove fertilizers and harmful substances.

> Be careful when using medications. Shrimps in particular cannot tolerate all the medications that can be used in aquariums.

> Hargreaves, Vincent. *The Complete Book of the Freshwater Aquarium: A Comprehensive Reference Guide to More Than 600 Freshwater Fish and Plants.* San Diego: Salamander Books, 2007.
> Smith, Mark. *Lake Tanganyika Cichlids.* Hauppauge, NY: Barron's Educational Series, Inc., 2008.
> Tullock, John. *Clownfish and Sea Anemones.* Hauppauge, NY: Barron's Educational Series, Inc., 1998.

Magazines

> Aquarium Fish International: *www.fishchannel.com/affc_portal.aspx*
> Freshwater and Marine Aquarium Magazine: *www.fishchannel.com/fama_portal.aspx*
> Tropical Fish Hobbyist: *www.tfhmagazine.com*

Web sites

> *http://freshaquarium.about.com:* Focus on freshwater aquariums.
> *www.aqua-fish.net:* A guide to tropical freshwater aquarium fish, plants, and biotopes.
> *http://naturalaquariums.com:* Information for planted aquariums, plus a forum for questions and answers.
> *http://fins.actwin.com:* The fish information service.
> *http://www.aquaristsonline.com:* Information on aquarium care and setup.

Photo Credits

Aquapress/Christian Piednoir: 20–1, 21–1; **Kai Arendt:** 35–2; **Dieter Bork:** 2–2, 22, 24, 26, 33–1, 35–1, 41–1, 55, Cover 8 r.; **Jakob Geck:** 21–2; **Martin Hallmann:** 40–3; **Karin Heckel-Merz:** 8; **Hippocampus**/Frank Teigler: 42, Cover 8 l.; **JBL**/online-Hospital: 56; **Burkhard Kahl:** Cover, 1, 4, 15, 20–3, 33–2, 35–3, 37–1, 37–3, 40–1, cover clap 3–3; **Christel Kasselmann:** 13–2, 18, 20–2, 21–3, 21–4, 21–5, 29–1; **Oliver Knott:** 6, 29–2; **Ingo Koslowski:** 44, cover 7–2; **Oliver Lucanus:** 37–2, 40–2, 41–3, 53; **Chris Lukhaup:** 2–1, 9, 12/13, 12–3, 19, 30, 39–1, 39–2, 39–3, 41–4, 41–5, 58, Cover 4–1, Cover 4–2, Cover 6, Cover 8 mid.; **Nonn Panitvong:** 25; **Armin Peither:** 3; **Michael Schlüter:** 13–1, Cover 3–2; **Heinz Schmidbauer:** 10–1, 10–2, 11–3, 11–4, 12–1, 12–2, 13–3, 14, 16, 17, 27–1, 27–2, 27–3, 29–3, 32, 34, 36, 38, 45–1, 45–2, 46, 48–1, 48–2, 50, 51–1, 51–2, 52, 54, 57, 59–1, 59–2, 64–1, Cover 7–1, Cover 7–3; **Erwin Schrami:** 41–2; **Jörg Vierke:** Cover 3–1; **Uwe Werner:** 33–3

Answers to Questions on Living Conditions

> Your local pet shop owner can answer many questions, and you can find all kinds of information by searching reputable sites on the Internet.

First edition translated from the German by Eric A. Bye.
English translation © Copyright 2010 by Barron's Educational
Series, Inc.
Original title of the book in German is *Nano-Aquarien*.
© Copyright 2008 by Gräfe und Unzer Verlag GmbH, Munich.

All inquiries should be addressed to:
Barron's Educational Series, Inc.
250 Wireless Boulevard
Hauppauge, NY 11788
www.barronseduc.com

ISBN-13: 978-0-7641-4428-8
ISBN-10: 0-7641-4428-6

Library of Congress Catalog Card No.: 2009033224

Library of Congress Cataloging-in-Publication Data
Geck, Jacob.
  [Nano-Aquarien. English]
  Nanoaquarium/ Jakob Geck and Ulrich Schliewen; [translated
from the German by Eric A. Bye].
      p. cm.
  Includes bibliographical references and index.
  ISBN-13: 978-0-7641-4428-8
  ISBN-10: 0-7641-4428-6
  1. Aquariums. 2. Aquarium fishes. 3. Aquarium plants.
I. Schliewen, Ulrich. II. Title.
SF457.3 G4513 2010
639.34—dc22   2009033224

PRINTED IN CHINA
9 8 7 6 5 4 3 2 1

The Authors

Jakob Geck has been involved with the
aquarium hobby nearly all his life and
discovered his love of nanoaquariums
more than thirty years ago. He has written about nanos and the fishes and
shrimps that live in them in many periodicals, and has also participated in
many conferences. For the past three
years, he has been the honorary director
of the aquarium installation of the State
Zoological Collection in Munich.

Ulrich Schliewen has been an aquarium
hobbyist since his childhood. As a fish
specialist (ichthyologist) at the State
Zoological Collection in Munich, he has
turned his hobby into his profession. He
has previously written many successful
aquarium handbooks for Gräfe und
Unzer Publishers.

SOS – What to Do?

Overfed?

PROBLEM Too much food fell from the container into the tank. **REMEDY** Use a hose to suck up about two thirds of the water and the leftover food on the bottom or floating on the surface. Then replace the missing amount with prepared water.

White Spots

PROBLEM The fishes have white spots on their body and fins and rub against things. **REMEDY** White spot disease has made an appearance. Special medications from a pet shop work well. Be sure to use them carefully according to the directions and continue the therapy as long as indicated.

Overheating in Summer

PROBLEM On hot days the nano reaches temperatures over 87°F (30°C)—plants and creatures suffer in the heat. **REMEDY** Let out two thirds of the water and carry the tank to a cooler place and operate it there. Replace the missing water.

Smear Algae

PROBLEM A slimy, musty smelling, dark green carpet of algae covers the plants, decorations, and substrate. **REMEDY** Patience is the only way to successfully deal with this. The cause—smear or blue algae—are not algae, but rather bacteria that take advantage of unstable aquarium conditions (e.g., after setting up a new aquarium). The coating is sucked up every day with an aquarium hose, and partial water changes are performed frequently with prepared water. Once the aquarium has stabilized after a couple of weeks, the algae usually disappear as quickly as they came. Unfortunately, there is no definite explanation for infestations of smear algae. In any case, you should avoid chemical preparations.

Strained Breathing

PROBLEM The fishes are struggling to breathe after a partial water change, even though the water is well aerated. **REMEDY** The old water was probably under too much strain from organic waste products because of an overly long interval in water changes or overfeeding. Do another water change of two thirds of the tank water. Fill the tank with prepared water.